super
simple quilts

#1

WITH ALEX ANDERSON
& LIZ ANELOSKI

9 Pieced Projects from Strips, Squares & Rectangles

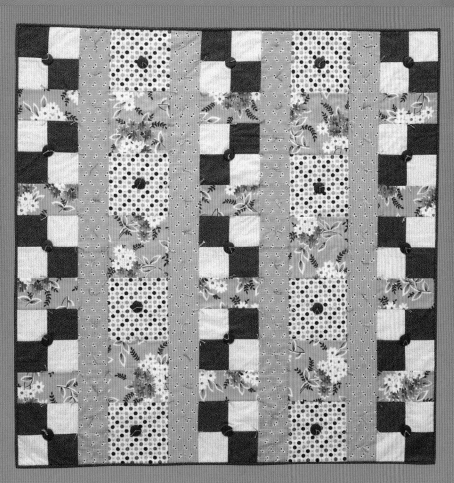

C&T PUBLISHING

Text copyright © 2008 by Alex Anderson and Liz Aneloski

Artwork copyright © 2008 by C&T Publishing, Inc.

Publisher: Amy Marson

Editorial Director: Gailen Runge

Acquisitions Editor: Jan Grigsby

Editor: Liz Aneloski

Technical Editors: Nanette S. Zeller and Sandy Peterson

Copyeditor/Proofreader: Wordfirm Inc.

Design Director/Cover & Book Designer: Christina D. Jarumay

Production Coordinator: Kirstie L. Pettersen and Kiera Lofgreen

Illustrator: John Heisch

Photography by Luke Mulks and Diane Pedersen of C&T
Publishing unless otherwise noted

Published by C&T Publishing, Inc., P.O. Box 1456, Lafayette, CA
94549

contents

acknowledgments

We'd like to thank Gayle Ronconi for her perfect piecing
of many of the quilts, the members of the C&T
Publishing editorial department for their ideas and inspi-
ration, and the following companies for providing the
wonderful buttons and fabrics used in the quilts:

Dill Buttons

Free Spirit

P&B Textiles

RJR Fashion Fabrics

Timeless Treasures Fabrics

introduction

These quilts can be first quilts for beginners or fast quilts for more experienced quilters looking for the perfect gift, donation, or baby quilt.

This book offers

3 quilt designs in

3 fabric styles in

3 sizes with

3 layer-securing methods and

3 binding techniques.

Choose the size of quilt you want, and from one materials list you can make any of the three quilt designs. This means you can choose a size, shop for fabric (photos of fabric swatches will help you), and then go home and decide which quilt design you want to make. Choose a securing method and binding technique, and you're done! See how easy?

We have included basic guidance to get you started and a great list of books (page 27) you can refer to if you want more information.

I often have the pleasure of brainstorming with Liz. I always treasure the time together. We each bring our own perspective to the table, and more often than not, they are keenly in sync. One such occasion was in the recent past. We were chatting about what sort of book was needed. As usual, life took its twists and turns, and that conversation was left on the back burner, or so I thought. Several months later I received a call from Liz and she wanted to show me "something." Bingo, her quilts hit the nail on the head. She asked if I would be interested in providing the general quiltmaking instructions for the book and before we knew it, Liz and I were co-authors! We are both very excited about this collaboration—fun, fast, simple projects, perfect for the beginner or the seasoned quilter who wants a quick project, in perfect C&T style.

-Alex

Over the many years that Alex and I have known each other, our relationship has developed through many different experiences: quilt show chairman and vendor, quilting friends/parents, editor and author, and now co-authors. The fun just never ends. With this book, we have combined Alex's expertise in quiltmaking knowledge, with my design and project writing skills. I hope you have fun with the simple designs, techniques, and many options that await you.

-Liz

the basics

 note See page 27 for sources of more detailed information.

essential supplies

■ **Sewing machine** (good working condition, with proper tension [refer to the manufacturer's guide for proper adjustment], an even stitch, and a good-quality size 80 needle)

■ 45mm **rotary cutter**

■ 17″ × 22″ self-healing **rotary cutting mat** (must be used with the rotary cutter)

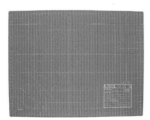

■ 6″ × 12″ **rotary cutting ruler**

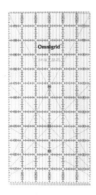

■ **Scissors** (small, for cutting threads)

■ **Pins** (thin, fine quilter's or silk pins work best)

■ **Sewing thread** (good-quality matching or neutral-color cotton)

■ **Seam ripper** (sharp, good quality)

■ **Iron**

■ **Safety pins** (1″ long for basting)

■ **Perle cotton or crochet cotton thread** (for tying and big-stitch hand quilting)

DMC perle cotton

Crochet cotton

■ **Needles** (darning or chenille needles with eyes large enough for the perle cotton for tying and big-stitch hand quilting)

■ **Buttons**

■ **Masking tape** (narrow width to mark quilting lines)

fabric

Use only high-quality 100% cotton fabric. Less expensive cottons can stretch and distort and be very frustrating to work with.

Always use a combination of light, medium, and dark fabrics in a variety of print sizes. This will result in interesting, exciting quilts.

rotary cutting

■ Practice and learn to use the rotary cutter safely and properly.

■ Cut accurately for accurate results.

■ Always close the safety latch on the rotary cutter after each cut.

■ Always cut away from your body, at a 90° angle.

■ Hold the rotary cutter as shown, with your index finger extended along the back of the cutter.

Left-handed

Right-handed

■ Place the side of the rotary cutter blade directly against the edge of the ruler.

Place the blade against the edge of the ruler.

1. Fold the fabric selvage (finished edge) to selvage, then fold again.

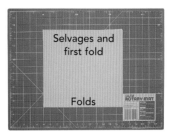

Fold the fabric twice.

2. Align a vertical line of the ruler with the bottom fold of the fabric. Trim to straighten and square up the raw edges.

Left-handed

Right-handed

3. Line up the vertical measurement on the ruler with the trimmed edge of the fabric. Cut the size and number of strips indicated in the charts included in the instructions for each project.

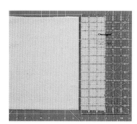
Left-handed

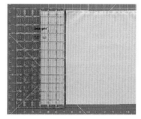
Right-handed

4. Rotate the mat and fabric. Trim off the uneven raw edges to square up the short edges. Line up the measurement on the ruler with the trimmed edge of the fabric. Cut the size and number of units (squares and rectangles) indicated in the charts included in the instructions for each project.

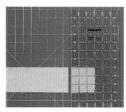
Left-handed

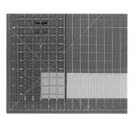
Right-handed

stitching

Straight stitching makes nice straight seamlines.

Use a stitch length just long enough that a seam ripper will slide nicely under the stitches. Backstitching is not necessary because all the seam ends will be enclosed by other seams.

¼˝ SEAM ALLOWANCE

Always use ¼˝ seam allowances for piecing the quilt tops. This is crucial for accurate results.

1. Raise the sewing machine needle and presser foot and place your rotary ruler under the needle.

2. Lower the presser foot, then manually ease the needle down on top of the ¼˝ mark.

3. Place a piece of masking tape along the edge of the ruler to mark ¼˝ on the throat plate to use as your seam guide.

4. Sew a sample to check to be sure you are sewing an exact ¼˝ seam allowance.

pinning

Pin at least the beginning and end of each seam. More pins make it easier to align the pieces when you sew.

When aligning seams that are pressed in opposite directions, place a pin on each side of the seam, no more than ⅛˝ from the seam.

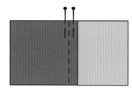

Place pins.

pressing

Press on a firm surface (an ironing board with a single pad).

Press the seams in one direction, not open, as follows:

Place the pieced unit on the ironing surface with the fabric you want the seam pressed toward on top, open the unit, and press. The seam should be pressed toward the correct fabric.

finishing the quilt

BATTING AND BACKING

Batting (low-loft polyester, approximately 2˝ larger than the quilt top on each side)

Backing (approximately 2˝ larger than the quilt top on each side)

If your quilt top is larger than one width of fabric, you will need to sew pieces of fabric together to make the backing (trim off the selvages first). If you're using leftover fabrics, sew pieces together to achieve the size listed in the Materials chart. You should have enough leftover fabrics from making the project quilts to use for backing and binding.

LAYERING

1. Place the backing wrong side up. Secure the backing to a large, flat surface, pulling the backing smooth and taut (not too tight). Use masking tape to secure on a table or hard floor or T-pins on nonloop carpet.

2. Place the batting on top of the backing and smooth out the wrinkles.

3. Smooth the quilt top onto the batting, right side up.

BASTING

Pin baste evenly across the quilt about every 3˝ with safety pins.

note If you plan your tying or quilting design before you pin baste, you can place the safety pins so they will not be in the way.

SECURING THE LAYERS

Securing Method #1: Tying

1. Decide whether you want the knots and tails to be on the front or the back of the quilt.

2. Thread a large-eyed needle with the tying thread. (The quilts in this book were tied with DMC perle cotton or crochet cotton thread.)

> *note* You can use a single or double thread, depending on how much you want the thread to show.

3. Push the needle through all 3 layers, so it comes out through the other side.

> *note* If you want the knots on the front, push the needle in from the front. If you want the knots on the back, push the needle in from the back.

4. Push the needle back through the layers, approximately ⅛″–¼″ from where it originally went through the layers. Pull the thread, leaving a 1½″–2″ tail.

5. Tie the knot as shown below. This knot is more secure than a square knot. Trim the thread ends to the length you want.

A. Tie a half-knot.

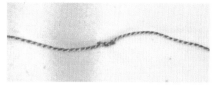
B. Pull it tight.

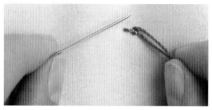
Left-handed

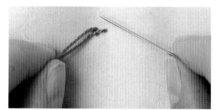
Right-handed

C. Hold the two strands and the needle as shown

Left-handed

Right-handed

D. Take the needle around the threads. Then, pull the needle through the loops.

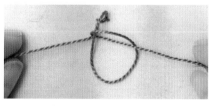
E. Let go of the thread end that is attached to the needle and hold only the short thread tail in your other hand.

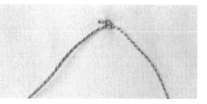
F. Pull the knot tight.

> *note* You can tie on buttons using this same method.

Securing Method #2:
Big-Stitch Hand Quilting

note It is not necessary to use a quilting hoop or frame when big-stitch hand quilting, but you have to be very careful not to pull the stitches too tight. You want your quilt to remain very flat and smooth.

The methods shown here for big-stitch hand quilting differ from traditional hand quilting methods because of the thickness of the thread and the size of the stitches.

1. Knot one end of the thread. (The quilts in this book were tied with either DMC perle cotton or crochet cotton thread.)

note Whenever possible, start and end the line of stitching at the edge of the quilt. This will hide the knots. If you have to start or stop the stitches in the middle of the quilt, make your knots as small as possible on the back of the quilt.

2. Insert the needle from the back of the quilt and pull the thread through to the front. Sew a running stitch, making the stitches approximately ¼″ long.

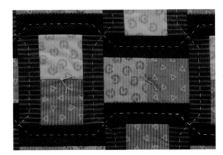

Running stitch

3. When you come to the end of the stitching or have approximately 6″ of thread left, knot the thread on the back of the quilt as shown below.

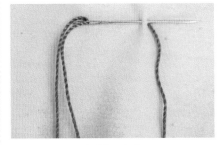

Left-handed   Right-handed

A. Take a tiny stitch through just the backing and batting.

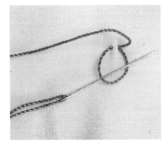 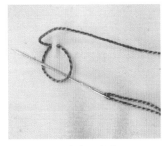 

Left-handed   Right-handed

B. Put the needle through the loop.   **C. Pull it tight.**

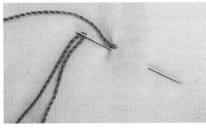 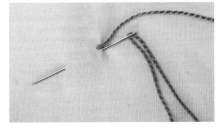

Left-handed   Right-handed

D. Run the needle through the backing and batting about ½″.

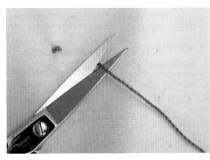 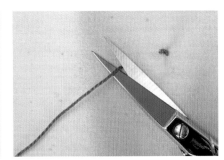

Left-handed   Right-handed

E. Trim off the thread where it exits the backing.

Method #3: Machine Quilting in the Ditch

This is a simple method of machine quilting in the ditch to get you started. Machine quilting takes practice.

note The larger the quilt, the more challenging it is to machine quilt.

■ You *must* use a walking/even-feed foot on your sewing machine for the layers to feed through the machine evenly.

■ Refer to the sewing machine manufacturer's instructions for thread tension guidance. Sew on a test piece of layered fabric, batting, and backing until you achieve the perfect thread tension.

■ Begin and end the lines of stitching using very tiny stitches.

■ Use a slightly longer stitch than you use for piecing.

■ Machine quilt long lines of stitches from one edge of the quilt to the other whenever possible, starting from the center and working out. Then, quilt the shorter lines to finish quilting around the blocks.

■ Stitch as close to the "ditch" as you can without stitching the adjoining fabric.

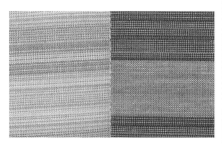

Stitch in the ditch.

BINDING

We recommend that you use left-over fabrics for binding. You can use 1 to 6 different fabrics. Look at the quilt photos throughout the book for ideas.

Binding Method #1: Squared Corners, Hand Finished on the Back

1. Trim the batting and backing even with the edges of the quilt top.

2. Cut as many 2¼″-wide strips as you need to go all the way around the quilt, plus 10″ or more extra.

3. Sew the strips together using diagonal seams to make 4 lengths at least 2″ longer than the edges of the quilt.

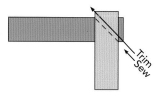

Piece the strips using diagonal seams. Trim.

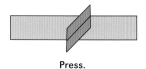

Press.

4. Measure the quilt width through the middle from side to side. Trim 2 binding strips the width of the quilt plus 1″.

5. Fold the strips in half lengthwise, wrong sides together, and press.

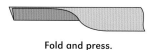

Fold and press.

6. Align the raw edges of the binding along the top edge of the front of the quilt. Let the binding extend ½″ past the corners of the quilt. Sew using a ¼″ seam allowance. Repeat for the bottom edge of the quilt.

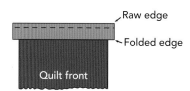

Sew the binding to the top and bottom edges of the quilt.

7. Flip the finished edge of the binding over the raw edge of the quilt and hand slipstitch the binding to the back of the quilt. Trim the ends even with the corners of the quilt.

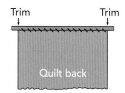

Fold the binding to the back, stitch, and trim.

8. Measure the quilt length through the middle from top to bottom. Trim 2 binding strips the length of the quilt plus 1″. Fold and press. Align and sew the strips as before, leaving ½″ of binding past the corners. Fold over the ends of the binding to create a finished edge before folding the binding to the back of the quilt. Hand slipstitch the binding, including the ends, in place.

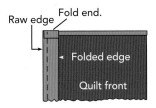

Fold the ends and stitch the side binding.

Binding Method #2: Squared Corners, Machine Finished on the Front

1. Follow Steps 1–5 for Binding Method #1, page 9.

2. Align the raw edges of the binding with the top edge of the back of the quilt. Let the binding extend ½″ past the corners of the quilt. Sew using a ¼″ seam allowance. Repeat for the bottom edge of the quilt.

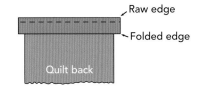

Sew the binding to the top edge of the quilt.

3. Flip the finished edge of the binding over the raw edge of the quilt and machine stitch to the front of the quilt using straight or decorative stitches. Trim the ends even with the edge of the quilt.

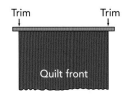

Fold the binding to the front, stitch, and trim.

4. Measure the quilt length through the middle from top to bottom. Trim 2 binding strips the length of the quilt plus 1″. Fold and press. Align and sew the strips to the back of the quilt as before, leaving ½″ of binding past the corners. Fold over the ends of the binding to create a finished edge before folding the binding to the front of the quilt. Machine stitch to the front of the quilt, as in Step 3.

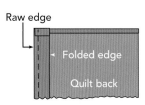

Fold the ends and stitch the side binding.

Binding Method #3: Mitered Corners, Hand Finished on the Back

1. Trim the batting and backing even with the edges of the quilt top.

2. Cut as many 2¼″-wide strips as you need to go all the way around the quilt, plus 10″ or more extra.

3. Sew the strips together using diagonal seams to make one long length.

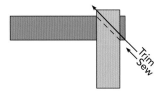

Piece the strips using diagonal seams. Trim.

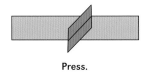

Press.

4. Fold the strips in half lengthwise, wrong sides together, and press.

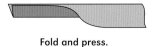

Fold and press.

5. With the raw edges of the quilt and binding aligned, pin the binding to the front of the quilt, beginning a few inches from a corner, leaving the first 6″ of the binding unattached. Start sewing, using a ¼″ seam allowance.

6. Stop ¼″ from the first corner of the quilt and backstitch one stitch.

Stitch ¼″ from a corner.

7. Lift the presser foot and needle. Rotate the quilt one-quarter turn. Fold the binding at a right angle so it extends straight above the quilt.

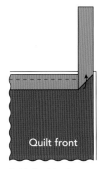

Fold the binding up.

8. Bring the binding down, even with the edge of the quilt. Begin sewing again at the folded edge, stopping ¼″ from the next corner and backstitching one stitch.

Fold down and stitch.

9. Repeat for all the sides of the quilt. Stop sewing 6″ from where you started.

10. Overlap the tails and trim, leaving a 2″ overlap.

11. Turn the beginning tail end under ¼″.

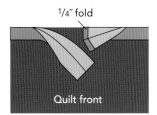

Turn the end under ¼″.

12. Place the ending tail end inside the beginning tail end.

Place the ending tail inside the beginning tail.

13. Adjust to the proper length, pin, and sew to finish the seam.

Pin, then sew.

14. Fold to the back of the quilt and hand stitch to finish.

Fold to the back and stitch.

marching in line

Marching in Line; New Retro by Liz Aneloski

Wall/Crib: 42½" × 42½"; 7 blocks/strip sets × 7 blocks/strip sets

Twin: 66½" × 90½"; 11 blocks/strip sets × 15 blocks/strip sets

Queen: 90½" × 102½"; 15 blocks/strip sets × 17 blocks/strip sets

Finished block size: 6" × 6"

materials

Yardages are based on 42"-wide fabric.

Fabric		Wall/Crib	Twin	Queen
Light		½ yard	⅞ yard	1¼ yards
Medium #1		½ yard	1 yard	1⅜ yards
Medium #2		½ yard*	1¼ yards	1¾ yards
Medium #3		½ yard*	1⅝ yards	2⅛ yards
Dark #1		⅝ yard	1⅔ yards	2¼ yards
Dark #2		⅝ yard*	1⅔ yards	2¼ yards
Backing		48" × 48" (Use leftovers and supplement, as necessary)	72" × 96" (Use leftovers and supplement, as necessary)	96" × 108" (Use leftovers and supplement, as necessary)
Binding		Leftovers** or ½ yard	Leftovers** or ⅔ yard	Leftovers** or ¾ yard
Batting		48" × 48"	72" × 96"	96" × 108"

* To avoid extra piecing, use fabric with at least 42½" usable width.

** There will be enough left over to create a multifabric binding.

cutting

Write the fabric name on masking tape and attach to each strip.

Fabric	Wall/Crib Size of Strips	Number of Strips	Twin Size of Strips	Number of Strips	Queen Size of Strips	Number of Strips
Light	3½" × fabric width	2	3½" × fabric width	7	3½" × fabric width	11
Medium #1	3½" × fabric width	3	3½" × fabric width	8	3½" × fabric width	12
Medium #2	3" × 42½" *	3	3" × fabric width	12	3" × fabric width	18
Medium #3	3" × 42½" *	3	3" × fabric width	12	3" × fabric width	18
Dark #1	3½" × fabric width	3	3½" × fabric width	8	3½" × fabric width	12
Dark #2	3½" × fabric width	2	3½" × fabric width	7	3½" × fabric width	11
	1½" × 42½" *	3	1½" × fabric width	12	1½" × fabric width	18

making the units and strip sets

Use a ¼″ seam allowance.

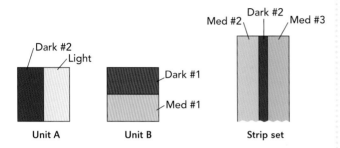

Unit A   Unit B   Strip set

1. Place a 3½″ light strip and a 3½″ dark #2 strip together with right sides together. Align and sew along one long edge. Press the seam allowance toward the dark fabric. Repeat with the remaining light and dark #2 strips for Unit A.

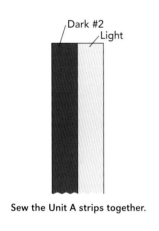

Sew the Unit A strips together.

2. Place a 3½″ medium #1 strip and a 3½″ dark #1 strip together with right sides together. Align and sew along one long edge. Press the seam allowance toward the dark fabric. Repeat with the remaining medium #1 and dark #1 strips for Unit B.

Sew the Unit B strips together.

3. Trim off the selvages from one edge of each Unit A and Unit B strip set. Beginning at this trimmed end, subcut each strip set into 6½″ units. Cut the number of units specified in the chart below.

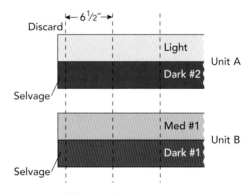

Subcut strip sets into units.

size and number of units

	Wall/Crib		Twin		Queen	
Fabric	Size of Units	Number of Units	Size of Units	Number of Units	Size of Units	Number of Units
Light/dark #2 strip sets (Unit A)	6½″ × 6½″	12	6½″ × 6½″	42	6½″ × 6½″	64
Medium #1/dark #1 strip sets (Unit B)	6½″ × 6½″	16	6½″ × 6½″	48	6½″ × 6½″	72
Medium #2 strip	3″ × 42½″	3	3″ × 90½″	5	3″ × 102½″	7
Dark #2 strip	1½″ × 42½″	3	1½″ × 90½″	5	1½″ × 102½″	7
Medium #3 strip	3″ × 42½″	3	3″ × 90½″	5	3″ × 102½″	7
Strip set	6½″ × 42½″	3	6½″ × 90½″	5	6½″ × 102½″	7

4. Piece (if necessary*) the medium #2, 1½″ dark #2, and medium #3 strips. Trim the selvage edges, sew the strips together end to end, and cut to make the number and length specified in the chart (page 14).

5. Place a 3″ medium #2 strip and a 1½″ dark #2 strip together with right sides together. Align and sew along the long edge. Press the seam allowance toward the dark fabric. Place a 3″ medium #3 strip on top of the dark #2 strip with right sides together. Align and sew along the long edge. Press the seam allowance toward the dark fabric. Repeat with the remaining medium #2, dark #2, and medium #3 strips to create the number of strip sets specified in the chart (page 14).

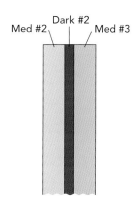

Med #2 Dark #2 Med #3

Sew the strip sets together.

constructing the quilt top

1. Sew alternating A and B units together to form vertical rows. Refer to the quilt construction illustration for the unit placement and number of rows. Press the seam allowances toward the A units.

2. Arrange the rows and strip sets, rotating and alternating them as shown.

3. Sew the rows together, pressing the seam allowances toward the strip sets.

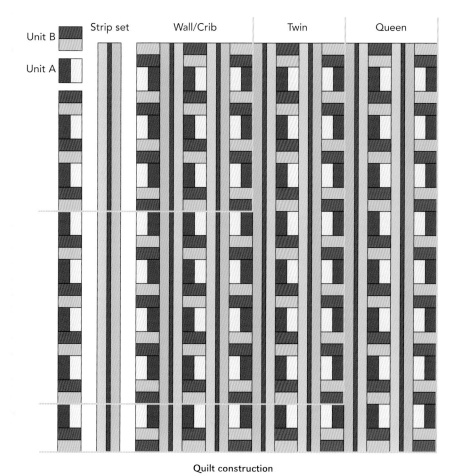

Quilt construction

finishing

Refer to Finishing the Quilt, beginning on page 6.

1. Layer and baste the quilt (page 6).

2. Choose a method to secure the layers (page 7).

3. Choose a binding technique (page 9).

Marching in Line; Traditional
by Liz Aneloski

Fabric		
Light		
Medium #1		
Medium #2		
Medium #3		
Dark #1		
Dark #2		

Fabric		
Light		
Medium #1		
Medium #2		
Medium #3		
Dark #1		
Dark #2		

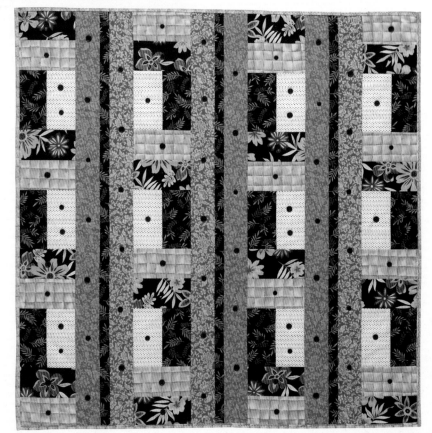

Marching in Line; Bright **by Liz Aneloski**

hopscotch

Hopscotch; Bright by Liz Ancloski

Wall/Crib: 42½″ × 42½″; 9 blocks/strips × 9 blocks/strips

Twin: 60½″ × 90½″; 13 blocks/strips × 20 blocks/strips

Queen: 78½″ × 96½″; 17 blocks/strips × 21 blocks/strips

Finished block size: 6″ × 6″

materials

Yardages are based on 42″-wide fabric.

Fabric		Wall/Crib	Twin	Queen
Light		½ yard	⅞ yard	1¼ yards
Medium #1		½ yard	1 yard	1⅜ yards
Medium #2		½ yard*	1¼ yards	1¾ yards
Medium #3		½ yard*	1⅝ yards	2⅛ yards
Dark #1		⅝ yard	1⅔ yards	2¼ yards
Dark #2		⅝ yard	1⅔ yards	2¼ yards
Backing		48″ × 48″ (Use leftovers and supplement, as necessary)	66″ × 96″ (Use leftovers and supplement, as necessary)	84″ × 102″ (Use leftovers and supplement, as necessary)
Binding		Leftovers** or ½ yard	Leftovers** or ⅔ yard	Leftovers** or ¾ yard
Batting		48″ × 48″	66″ × 96″	84″ × 102″

* To avoid extra piecing, use fabric with at least 42½″ usable width.

** There will be enough left over to create a multifabric binding.

cutting

Write the fabric name on masking tape and attach to each strip.

Fabric	Wall/Crib		Twin		Queen	
	Size of Strips	Number of Strips	Size of Strips	Number of Strips	Size of Strips	Number of Strips
Light	3½″ × fabric width	3	3½″ × fabric width	8	3½″ × fabric width	10
Medium #1	3½″ × 42½″ *	2	3½″ × fabric width	7	3½″ × fabric width	10
Medium #2	3½″ × 42½″ *	2	3½″ × fabric width	7	3½″ × fabric width	10
Medium #3	3½″ × fabric width	2	3½″ × fabric width	7	3½″ × fabric width	9
	6½″ × fabric width	1	6½″ × fabric width	4	6½″ × fabric width	6
Dark #1	3½″ × fabric width	3	3½″ × fabric width	8	3½″ × fabric width	10
Dark #2	6½″ × fabric width	2	6½″ × fabric width	4	6½″ × fabric width	6

making the four-patch blocks and strip sets

Use a ¼″ seam allowance.

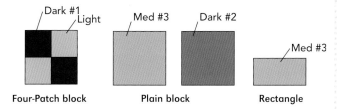

| Four-Patch block | Plain block | Rectangle |

1. To make the Four-Patch blocks, place a 3½″ light strip and a 3½″ dark #1 strip together with right sides together. Align and sew along one long edge. Press the seam allowance toward the dark fabric. Repeat with the remaining light and dark #1 strips.

Sew the strips together.

2. Trim off the selvages from one edge of each strip set. Beginning at this trimmed end, subcut the strip set into 3½″ units. Cut the number of 3½″ × 6½″ units specified in the chart below.

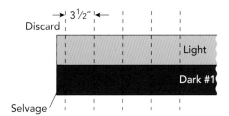

Subcut the strip sets into units.

3. Place 2 units together with right sides together, alternating the units as shown. The seam allowances should be facing in opposite directions so the seamlines will align perfectly. Pin in place (see Pinning, page 6).

Pin the units together.

4. Sew along the pinned edge. Press. Repeat to make the number of blocks shown in the chart below.

Four-Patch block

size and number of units

Fabric	Wall/Crib		Twin		Queen	
	Size of Units	Number of Units [Number of Blocks]	Size of Units	Number of Units [Number of Blocks]	Size of Units	Number of Units [Number of Blocks]
Light/dark #1 strip sets	3½″ × 6½″	30 [15]	3½″ × 6½″	80 [40]	3½″ × 6½″	110 [55]
Medium #1	3½″ × 42½″	2	3½″ × 90½″	3	3½″ × 96½″	4
Medium #2	3½″ × 42½″	2	3½″ × 90½″	3	3½″ × 96½″	4
Medium #3	3½″ × 6½″	12	3½″ × 6½″	40	3½″ × 6½″	50
	6½″ × 6½″	6	6½″ × 6½″	21	6½″ × 6½″	32
Dark #2	6½″ × 6½″	8	6½″ × 6½″	24	6½″ × 6½″	32

5. Trim the selvage edges, then subcut the 3½″ medium #3 strips into 3½″ × 6½″ rectangles to make the number specified in the chart (page 19).

6. Trim the selvage edges, then subcut the 6½″ medium #3 and dark #2 strips into 6½″ squares to make the number specified in the chart (page 19).

7. Piece (if necessary*) the medium #1 and medium #2 strips. Trim the selvage edges, sew the strips together end to end, and cut to make the number and length strips specified in the chart (page 19).

constructing the quilt top

1. Sew alternating Four-Patch blocks and medium #3 rectangles together to form vertical rows. Refer to the quilt construction illustration for the piece placement and number of rows. Press the seam allowances toward the medium #3 rectangles.

2. Sew alternating dark #2 squares and medium #3 squares together. Refer to the quilt construction illustration for the square placement and number of rows. Press the seam allowances toward the dark squares.

3. Arrange the pieced rows and medium #1 and medium #2 strips as shown.

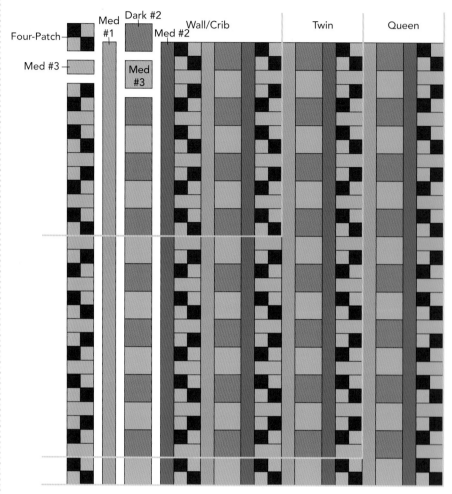

Quilt construction

4. Sew the rows and strips together, pressing the seam allowances toward the strips.

finishing

Refer to Finishing the Quilt, beginning on page 6.

1. Layer and baste the quilt (page 6).

2. Choose a method to secure the layers (page 7).

3. Choose a binding technique (page 9).

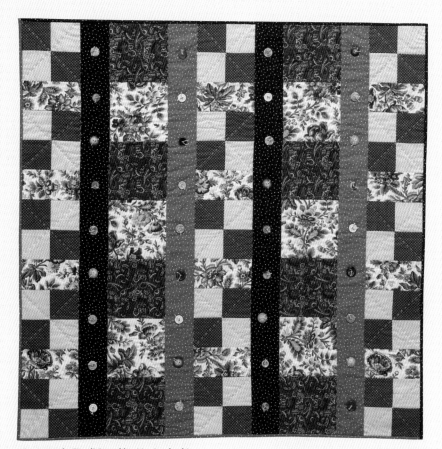

Hopscotch; Traditional by Liz Aneloski

Fabric		
Light		
Medium #1		
Medium #2		
Medium #3		
Dark #1		
Dark #2		

Fabric		
Light		
Medium #1		
Medium #2		
Medium #3		
Dark #1		
Dark #2		

Hopscotch; New Retro by Liz Aneloski

twist and turn

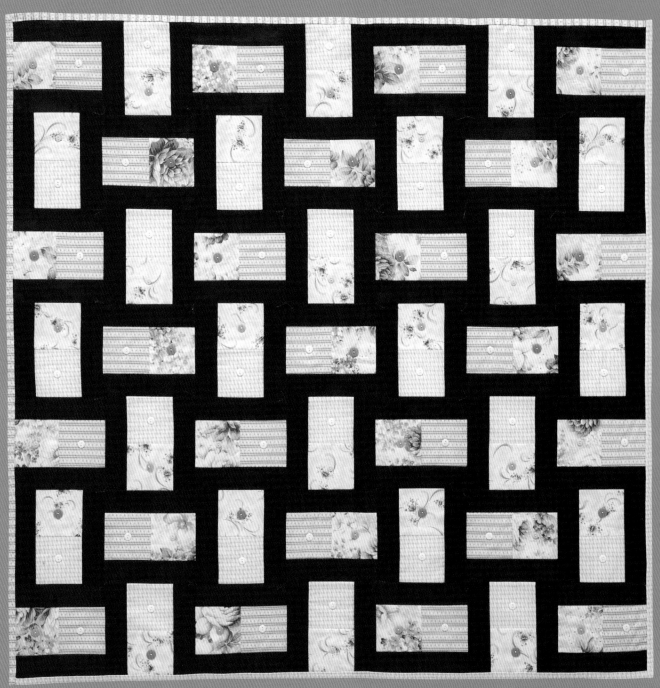

Twist and Turn; Traditional pieced by Gayle Ronconi and designed, tied, and bound by Liz Aneloski

Wall/Crib: 42½" × 42½"; 7 blocks × 7 blocks

Twin: 66½" × 90½"; 11 blocks × 15 blocks

Queen: 84½" × 96½"; 14 blocks × 16 blocks

Finished block size: 6" × 6"

materials

Yardages are based on 42"-wide fabric.

Fabric	Wall/Crib	Twin	Queen
Light	½ yard	⅞ yard	1¼ yards
Medium #1	½ yard	1 yard	1⅜ yards
Medium #2	½ yard	1¼ yards	1¾ yards
Medium #3	½ yard	1⅝ yards	2⅛ yards
Dark #1	⅝ yard	1⅔ yards	2¼ yards
Dark #2	⅝ yard	1⅔ yards	2¼ yards
Backing	48" × 48" (Use leftovers and supplement, as necessary)	72" × 96" (Use leftovers and supplement, as necessary)	90" × 102" (Use leftovers and supplement, as necessary)
Binding	Leftovers** or ⅜ yard	Leftovers** or ⅝ yard	Leftovers** or ¾ yard
Batting	48" × 48"	72" × 96"	90" × 102"

** There will be enough left over to create a multifabric binding.

cutting

Write the fabric name on masking tape and attach to each strip.

Fabric	Wall/Crib		Twin		Queen	
	Size of Strips	Number of Strips	Size of Strips	Number of Strips	Size of Strips	Number of Strips
Light	3½" × fabric width	3	3½" × fabric width	8	3½" × fabric width	11
Medium #1	3½" × fabric width	3	3½" × fabric width	8	3½" × fabric width	11
Medium #2	3½" × fabric width	3	3½" × fabric width	8	3½" × fabric width	11
Medium #3	3½" × fabric width	3	3½" × fabric width	8	3½" × fabric width	11
Dark #1	2" × fabric width	8	2" × fabric width	28	2" × fabric width	38
Dark #2	2" × fabric width	9	2" × fabric width	28	2" × fabric width	38

making the blocks

Use a ¼″ seam allowance.

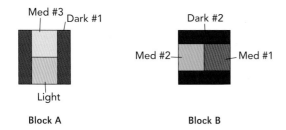

Block A

Block B

1. Place a light strip and a medium #3 strip together with right sides together. Align and sew along one long edge. Press the seam allowance toward the medium fabric. Repeat with the remaining light and medium #3 strips for Block A.

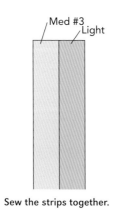

Sew the strips together.

2. Place a medium #1 strip and a medium #2 strip together with right sides together. Align and sew along one long edge. Press the seam allowance toward the darker fabric. Repeat with the remaining medium #1 and medium #2 strips for Block B.

Sew the strips together.

3. Trim off the selvages from one edge of each strip set. Beginning at this trimmed end, subcut the strip set into 3½″ units. Cut the number of units specified in the chart below.

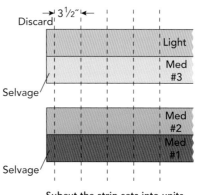

Subcut the strip sets into units.

size and number of units

Fabric	Wall/Crib		Twin		Queen	
	Size of Units	Number of Units [Number of Blocks]	Size of Units	Number of Units [Number of Blocks]	Size of Units	Number of Units [Number of Blocks]
Light/medium #3 strip sets (for Block A)	3½″ × 6½″	24 [24]	3½″ × 6½″	82 [82]	3½″ × 6½″	112 [112]
Medium #1/medium #2 strip sets (for Block B)	3½″ × 6½″	25 [25]	3½″ × 6½″	83 [83]	3½″ × 6½″	112 [112]
Dark #1 (for Block A)	2″ × 6½″	48	2″ × 6½″	164	2″ × 6½″	224
Dark #2 (for Block B)	2″ × 6½″	50	2″ × 6½″	166	2″ × 6½″	224

4. Trim the selvage edges, then subcut the dark #1 and dark #2 strips into 2″ × 6½″ rectangles to make the number specified in the chart (page 24).

5. Align, as shown, and sew dark #1 rectangles to each side of a light/medium #3 unit. Press the seam allowances toward the dark rectangles. Repeat to make the number of A blocks shown in the chart (page 24).

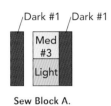

Sew Block A.

6. Align and sew dark #2 rectangles to each side of the medium #1/medium #2 units. Press the seam allowances toward the dark rectangles. Make the number of B blocks shown in the chart (page 24).

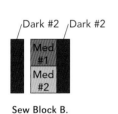

Sew Block B.

constructing the quilt top

1. Sew alternating A and B blocks together. Refer to the quilt construction illustration for the block placement and number of vertical rows. Press the seam allowances up on row 1, down on row 2, up on row 3, and so on.

2. Sew the rows together, pressing the seam allowances in the same direction.

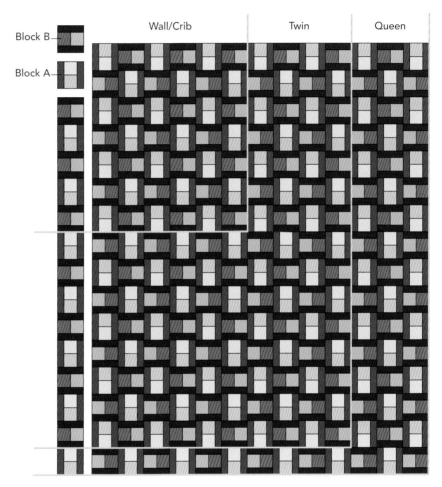

Quilt construction

finishing

Refer to Finishing the Quilt, beginning on page 6.

1. Layer and baste the quilt (page 6).

2. Choose a method to secure the layers (page 7).

3. Choose a binding technique (page 9).

Fabric		
Light		
Medium #1		
Medium #2		
Medium #3		
Dark #1		
Dark #2		

Twist and Turn; New Retro pieced by
Gayle Ronconi and designed, quilted,
and bound by Liz Aneloski

Fabric		
Light		
Medium #1		
Medium #2		
Medium #3		
Dark #1		
Dark #2		

Twist and Turn; Bright pieced by Gayle Ronconi, quilted by
Teresa Stroin, and designed and bound by Liz Aneloski

For more information, ask for a free catalog:

C&T Publishing
P.O. Box 1456
Lafayette, CA 94549

(800) 284-1114

email: ctinfo@ctpub.com
website: www.ctpub.com

For quilting supplies:

Cotton Patch
1025 Brown Ave.
Lafayette, CA 94549

(800) 835-4418 or
(925) 283-7883

email: CottonPa@aol.com
website: www.quiltusa.com

other books by Alex:

other books by Liz:

Great Titles
from C&T PUBLISHING

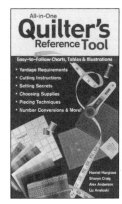

have three s
the fu
making these
super-easy quilts

- ■ 3 quilts, each in 3 sizes, with 3 fabric styles to choose from—the hardest part is choosing which one to make first!

- ▨ One supply list makes any of the quilts

- ■ Perfect first quilts for beginners—clear instructions and photos guide you from start to finish

- ▨ Perfect fast quilts for experienced quilters—simple patterns go together in a snap for charity quilts or gifts

Use this chart to make ANY quilt in this book!

Fabric	Wall/Crib	Twin	Queen
Light	½ yard	⅞ yard	1¼ yards
Medium #1	½ yard	1 yard	1⅜ yards
Medium #2	½ yard	1¼ yards	1¾ yards
Medium #3	½ yard	1⅝ yards	2⅛ yards
Dark #1	⅝ yard	1⅔ yards	2¼ yards
Dark #2	⅝ yard	1⅔ yards	2¼ yards

The Giggle Box

written by Patricia Schoch
illustrated by Lisa Lowell